Bach
for Recorder and Guitar
(SOPRANO-or-TENOR)

Arranged by
EUGENE REICHENTHAL

Contents

EDWARD B. Marks Music Company / HAL•LEONARD CORPORATION
7777 W. BLUEMOUND RD. P.O. BOX 13819 MILWAUKEE, WI 53213

EXCLUSIVELY DISTRIBUTED BY

This book is dedicated to Monica Dewey and Doris Hunter, who for many years have been playing recorder and guitar together for children of British schools.

FOREWORD

All the included selections are arranged to be played on a C recorder, either soprano (descant) or tenor, with guitar, but the upper line may quite effectively be carried by a flute, oboe or violin, and the guitar parts may be played by harpsichord or piano.

I have chosen the C recorders rather than the altos (trebles) in F for two reasons. There is a vast literature for alto recorders, but a comparative scarcity of fine solo or duet material for tenors and sopranos. And those keys in which the C recorders sound the best happen also to be the keys best suited to the guitar.

Few ornaments have been added editorially, but certain standard embellishments that were expected from Baroque performers have been written into the recorder part.

Ornaments may be sparingly improvised by those who are certain of the idiom, but such ornaments must conform with the mood of the selection and must not disturb the flow of the melodic line.

Trills are to be started on the beat with the upper note as an expressive, dissonant appoggiatura. Occasionally the appoggiatura is actually written in, and in such instances it would not be played again.

I hope that in making the changes necessary for a transcription I have succeeded in retaining the beauty, style and spirit of the original selection.

Eugene Reichenthal

March in G *from "The Little Note Book of Anna Magdalena Bach"*

Johann Sebastian Bach
Arranged by Eugene Reichenthal

Minuet

Johann Sebastian Bach
Arranged by Eugene Reichenthal

Wie soll Ich *from "Cantata 152"*

Johann Sebastian Bach
Arranged by Eugene Reichenthal

6

Prelude *from "18 Little Preludes and Fugues, No. 10"*
Johann Sebastian Bach
Arranged by Eugene Reichenthal

Sinfonia *from "Cantata 156"*
Johann Sebastian Bach
Arranged by Eugene Reichenthal

*The trill on B♭ is fingered:

On many recorders a better high B♭ than the
one given on standard fingering charts is

Minuet *from "French Suite No. 2"*

Johann Sebastian Bach
Arranged by Eugene Reichenthal

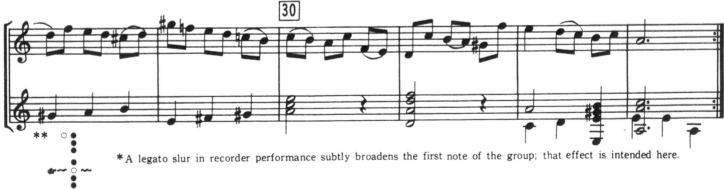

*A legato slur in recorder performance subtly broadens the first note of the group; that effect is intended here.

Minuet *from "French Suite No. 6"*

Johann Sebastian Bach
Arranged by Eugene Reichenthal

Recorder

Guitar

Bourrée in E minor

Johann Sebastian Bach
Arranged by Eugene Reichenthal

Gavotte *from "French Suite No. 5"*

Johann Sebastian Bach
Arranged by Eugene Reichenthal

Siciliano *from "Sonata No. 2 for Flute and Harpsichord"*

Johann Sebastian Bach
Arranged by Eugene Reichenthal

Bourrée in A minor

Johann Sebastian Bach

Arranged by Eugene Reichenthal

Jesu, Joy of Man's Desiring. *from "Cantata 147"*

Johann Sebastian Bach
Arranged by Eugene Reichenthal

Wisset ihr nicht *from "Cantata 154"*

Johann Sebastian Bach
Arranged by Eugene Reichenthal

Little Prelude *from "6 Little Preludes"*

Johann Sebastian Bach
Arranged by Eugene Reichenthal

Polonaise *from "The Little Note Book of Anna Magdalena Bach"*

Johann Sebastian Bach
Arranged by Eugene Reichenthal

Air in G

Johann Sebastian Bach
Arranged by Eugene Reichenthal